Nip it! Dig it!

Written by Natasha Paul

Collins

T0382112

Tig nips at it.

3

Sid digs a pit.

Sid

a pit

dig

Tad naps on Tom.

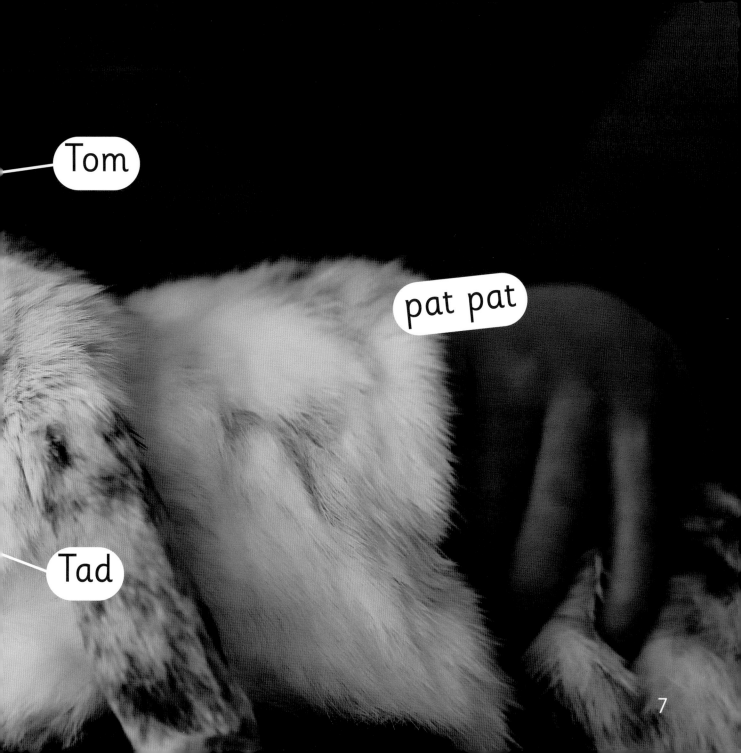

Tog sits. Tog sips.

Tog

a pot

dots

9

Pip sits on top.

Pip nips a pod.

Pog naps in it.

Nap in a pot!

13

14

🐾 Review: After reading 🐾

Use your assessment from hearing the children read to choose any GPCs, words or tricky words that need additional practice.

Read 1: Decoding

- Turn to page 2. Ask the children to sound out the letters in the word **nips**. (*n/i/p/s – **nips***) Check they don't miss the last "s".
- On pages 4 and 5, focus on the words **Sid**, **digs** and **pit**. Ask the children to sound out and blend each word, checking they don't muddle the end sound.
- Look at the "I spy sounds" pages (14–15). Point to the log and say: I spy an /o/ in log. Challenge the children to point to and name different things they can see containing the /o/ sound. (e.g. *pod, pot, box, dots, Tog, orange, tomatoes, hopping, rocks*)

Read 2: Prosody

- Model reading each page with expression to the children. After you have read each page, ask the children to have a go at reading with expression.

Read 3: Comprehension

- For every question ask the children how they know the answer. Ask:
  - On page 6, what is the rabbit called? (*Tad*)
  - On pages 8 and 9, what is Tog doing? (e.g. *drinking/sipping water from a pot*)
  - On pages 10 and 11, where is Pip and what is he doing? (e.g. *He is on top of a log and eating a peapod.*)
  - Which rabbits nip? Which rabbit digs? (*Tig and Pip*; *Sid*)
  - Which is your favourite rabbit? Why?